A BETTER CUSTOMER SERVICE ENVIRONMENT

Brian Rowland

Copyright © 2017 by Brian Rowland.

All rights reserved. No part of this publication may be reproduced, distributed or transmitted in any form or by any means, including photocopying, recording, or other electronic or mechanical methods, without the prior written permission of the publisher, except in the case of brief quotations embodied in critical reviews and certain other noncommercial uses permitted by copyright law. For permission requests, write to the author, at the website below.

Although the author has made every effort to ensure that the information in this book was correct at press time, the author does not assume and hereby disclaim any liability to any party for any loss, damage, or disruption caused by errors or omissions, whether such errors or omissions result from negligence, accident, or any other cause. The author tried to recreate events, locales and conversations from my memories of them. In order to maintain their anonymity in some instances he has changed the names of individuals and places, he may have changed some identifying characteristics and details such as physical properties, and occupations.

Printed and bound in the United States of America
www.butlerexperience.com

The Butler Experience/ Brian Rowland. —1st ed.
ISBN-978-0-692-86147-9

To my children, Xander and Katie who mean the world to me.

To Mom and Dad, thanks for all the support and pushing me forward all of these years.

Special thanks to Kathy- Without your support and guidance this would have never happen.

Thank You!

Contents

Introduction to the Butler Experience 1

Why Butlers in the Organization 5

Meeting The Butler 17

Be Serving At All Times 22

Use Your Knowledge 37

Trustworthy Service 49

Leadership 59

Empowerment 74

Relationships 85

Butler Culture 95

Bibliography 99

Index 106

About Author 109

CHAPTER 1

Introduction to the Butler Experience

I wrote The Butler Experience for one primary reason: bad customer service can be destructive – and financially detrimental – to any business or organization. Whether Direct-to-Consumer or Business-to-Business, we all know that the lack of good customer service plagues organizations worldwide.

Here in the U.S., the economic impact is staggering to businesses. An article, Bad Customer Service Costs Businesses Billions of Dollars, posted on forbes.com on August 27, 2016, reported that "Businesses are losing $62 billion per year through poor customer service. That's up $20 billion since 2013, just three years ago!" That's a compelling statistic!

A report, "Customers 2020," compiled by Walker Consulting of Indianapolis agrees, stating that "customers know more, and expect more." The report also indicated that 50 percent of the study respondents believe that by 2020, the experiences a company delivers to customers will be key to creating a competitive advantage for that business.

Today's heavy reliance upon and usage of social media platforms adds fuel to the fire. Customers have numerous online forums at their immediate disposal to share a negative customer service experience with the world – and they will use them.

While companies understand that customer service comes with challenges and opportunities, there is often a struggle in developing, implementing and maintaining a successful internal customer service culture to overcome the challenges and embrace the opportunities. This book seeks to help businesses and customer service staff prepare for new trends and expectations.

Good customer service is not a new issue to write about and in fact, there are numerous books on this subject suggesting a wealth of information exists. After reviewing several of these books, however, my conclusion is that books on the market describe what excellent customer service IS, but do not provide the tools and resources to build and develop the necessary hands-on skills that enhance customer service.

The Butler Experience seeks to help individuals and their organizations change that. The book is based on a true story about an employee who changed the way an organization provides customer service to its clientele. He elevated his employer's company from good to exceptional customer service simply by being a man committed to learning, doing his best and providing the best possible service to others, both personally and professionally. Below is an excerpt about Steven, my inspiration for this book.

I first met Steven in 2010 at an auto show in Chicago. At that time, he was working for a vendor at the show. Steven was in his late 20s, a rather unique-looking individual with spiked hair and the sides of his head were shaved. Despite a non-traditional appearance, he was one of the most humble and polite individuals I ever met. When he addressed others, it was always initially "Ma'am" or "Sir." He postured himself similar to a butler, standing with his hands behind his back, always pleasant and looking directly at the person he was talking with.

In 2013, Steven accepted a position within our organization. From the start, Steven did everything with excellence, working however long it took to get the job done. He was always willing to serve, always seeking to enhance his skills and knowledge – and when he made a promise or commitment, it was kept.

Steven's commitment to service and style not only quickly endeared him to his fellow team members and customers, but earned him a nickname of "The Butler." He was without question an empowered individual and leader who earned a lot of trust from his fellow employees and the customers. His skills and commitment to an excellent customer experience changed the customer service culture at our organization.

Steven would give the shirt off his back for someone in need. It is to honor him and his legacy of caring, compassion and *commitment in writing this book, The Butler Experience.*

-Brian Rowland

CHAPTER 2

Why Butlers in the Organization

Throughout the years, the role of a butler who keeps life running smoothly has been portrayed on popular weekly television series or in movies. I personally remember watching great television shows such as Mr. Belvedere or The Fresh Prince of Bel-Air with my family when I was younger. Like so many others, I often daydreamed that someday I would have a butler to take care of my home and family. Of course, that dream never became reality for me personally.

What happened instead was a chance meeting of this unique and wonderful individual, Steven, who displayed the qualities of a butler within my professional world. While he was not an employee of mine at first, he did subsequently accept a position within my company, where he had a significant and positive impact on his fellow workers and our customers. Steven's demeanor was not subservient; rather, he was a role model in professionalism and in caring about the customer, and delivering the best service possible. He consistently took customer service to the highest level. Steven's commitment and skills provided me with a clear strategy on how to improve our organization's customer service environment system-wide by developing our employees into butlers.

Like many other companies world-wide, our organization was faced with an ever-changing economy and I began to see a shift not only in how we did business, but a trend towards a negative impact on the bottom line. While business costs were rising, sales were not growing. Furthermore, income remained flat and often inconsistent from year to year. Employees were asked to take on added responsibility – and this resulted in a staff that was obviously overworked, exhausted and frustrated. Additionally, our customer service reputation suffered as we became more focused on getting the job done rather than giving customers the service experience they wanted and expected. Customers began to express their dissatisfaction, and we knew that improving our customer service environment needed to happen sooner than later.

Our company was not unique in this matter. Today's heavy reliance upon and usage of social media platforms has worsened the issue as consumers and business to business customers have numerous online forums through which to share negative customer service experiences with the world.

An Entrepreneur report cites that U.S. enterprises lose an estimated $83.3 billion annually due to poor customer service. The report states that nearly 64 percent of consumers believe that good customer service is more important than cost when considering which company to do business with. Furthermore, 55 percent of those responding said they would be willing to pay more to make sure they get better service.

While organizations understand that providing good customer service comes with challenges and opportunities, there is also often a struggle in developing, implementing and maintaining a successful internal customer service culture that can overcome the challenges and embrace the opportunities. A report issued by Walker Consulting of Indianapolis also indicates that good customer service is an expectation of what should be the norm and not the exception, stating that "customers know more and expect more." The report also indicated that 50 percent of the study respondents believe that by 2020, the experiences a company delivers to customers will be key to creating a competitive advantage for that business.

The butler concept provides the experience that customers need now and in the future. Developing butlers is critical to an organization's success now more than ever, and will help your organization prepare for new trends and meet expectations in the future.

Steven, who years ago had been fondly named The Butler by clients and his fellow employees, was the impetus to making these changes within my organization. I began to incorporate traits I observed from his style of service, skills and technique into our customer service training, even retraining existing staff and thus the butler was born within my organization.

Incorporating the butler concept into our culture made further sense to me after studying the history of a butler. After all, who best to ensure good customer service than the individual stereotypically perceived as one committed to serving – the butler?

The title of butler was typically given to an individual who was in charge of a wine cellar and handled the dispensing of liquor in the Victorian Age. This position evolved and the butler was then expected to perform the duties of the person known as a wine steward in the earlier Elizabethan Era – the time of Queen Elizabeth I and William Shakespeare. Over the next centuries, the butler position further evolved from a middle-ranked servant to being the senior-most servant in a household.

In modern times, the position of butler continued to transition into a modern-day role of responsibility in which the butler is acknowledged as the chief manager of the household. Butlers today are viewed as multi-faceted, knowledgeable, skilled and empowered professionals, with a true commitment to providing top-notch customer service.

Imagine if your company focused on helping employees hone those skills listed above and could improve customer service by building butlers within your professional environment. No, not a butler to manage your day and make home or office run smoothly; rather a customer service butler who knows the importance of quality service and professionalism – and that good or bad, the quality of customer service will affect any organization's bottom line.

At the risk of being redundant, again, who better to be a customer service role model than the butler? Butlers are knowledgeable about the employer's goals and expectations, are team-focused, ready and able to serve, and empowered. The butler philosophy and commitment is logically and easily integrated into an innovative business culture and staff training, designed to elevate the company's customer service to the highest levels. It would not only change your way of thinking, but the way the organization views customer service. Developing good butlers also creates strong ambassadors of your organization. Butlers play a significant role as ambassadors in many ways:

THEY KNOW THE ORGANIZATION

Butlers fully understand and oversee the vision of the organization; they are focused on successfully propelling the organization forward through integration and promotion of the vision.

Great success comes when your entire staff – from top to bottom – is focused on accomplishing the vision. Southwest Airlines is a good example of how employees who have a clear understanding of the company vision can help their company be an industry leader, as Southwest Airlines has been for more than 40 years. According to Forbes, Southwest Airlines' success is the result of ingraining a common core belief in all employees, including the company executives and pilots: to work together for a common purpose of giving exceptional service, and integrating that purpose in their customer interactions every day. Incorporating a similar customer service vision will help your organization's butlers provide world-class customer service every day through their interactions with your customers.

THEY ARE MORE ENGAGED

Butlers are engaged in the success of the organization, and are motivated to achieve the goals and values of the organization. Strong employees are positioned to have a strong influence on the organization. At the same time, the successful organization empowers its employees to make decisions, especially during tough times. Engaged and empowered employees are more eager and able to share the organization's culture with consumers, partners and vendors. Dale Carnegie Training shows that companies that engage their employees outperform other companies by up to 202 percent.

THEY CULTIVATE RELATIONSHIPS

Butlers build trust and relationships with your clients, co-workers, and management. These relationships are further based on accountability, collaboration, engagement and innovation. Trust is formed both internally and externally –

and strong relationships based on trust will be lasting relationships.

THEY DEMONSTRATE PASSION FOR WHAT THEY DO

Passion translates into results. Butlers who are passionate about their organization spread a positive vibe and the service culture becomes stronger in the organization. As discussed in a Gallup Poll, the best organizations hire and develop employees who are passionate about their work and who do whatever they can to engage and help their customers.

Learning how to develop butlers will help identify common gaps in an organization's customer service culture. The method is achieved simply by gaining an understanding of how butlers do it well and what their skillsets are, and then translating those skills into all levels of staff training within your business environment, specifically the customer service areas. Implementing the information and resources contained within The Butler Experience into your organization will make your company stronger, and help it become a customer service leader in your industry.

The premise for success is to first embrace and understand the BUTLER concept. The next actions are to then develop and implement the steps needed to change and improve a lagging customer service culture into one that maintains a competitive edge. While there can be numerous ways to form a team into butlers, the following six principles can make an immediate and dramatic change in your customer service. They did for me! It is known as the Butler acronym.

BE SERVING AT ALL TIMES

Most organizations fail to focus on the importance of serving at all times. Furthermore, employees are often not developed with sufficient additional training that prepares them to anticipate and meet customer needs. Untrained employees tend to wait to be asked by the customer; that can be too late, resulting in an unhappy (and perhaps lost) customer. Consider the following questions:
- How can we best serve our customers all the time?
- How can we demonstrate our willingness to service?

USE YOUR KNOWLEDGE

Job-specific knowledge is the missing element in many organizations, as employers often place new hires into positions with little or no experience. An interesting fact shared by Deloitte Consulting LLP shows that 70 percent of training occurs informally on the job.

On-the-job training is one of many reasons that good customer service is lacking in organizations. Enhancing their employee's development in a specific knowledge area is essential to an organization's success. Organizations that develop knowledgeable employees are seen as leaders in their industry. Consider the following questions:

- Does our organization/staff have the knowledge?
- How do we enhance our knowledge?

TRUSTWORTHY SERVICE

Relationships are built on trust. How many times do organizations over-promise and under-deliver? I think it happens more today than ever before. Most likely, it happens more than an organization realizes until suddenly, it is too late and there are problems. Organizations are not meeting expectations, and there is no consistency. Robert Eckert, former chairman of Mattel, once said: "As you go to work, your responsibility should be to build trust." Trustworthy service is about being you around your customer. Consider the following questions:

- Do our customers trust us?
- How do we enhance trust?

LEADERSHIP

The ability to take customer service to the next level means creating leaders within your organization. It is also about developing staff into ambassadors who will exemplify the characteristics of excellent customer service. Leadership is an area that can be tough for individuals and organizations to recognize. Consider the following questions:

- Do we demonstrate we are leaders in the industry?
- How do we build leaders?

Empower

Empowering employees can be a constant struggle for managers and organizations, particularly when a supervisor has a hard time letting go of the reins and not feeling like he or she is giving up power by empowering. The benefit of empowering employees is that it allows them to create long-term relationships with your existing and potential customer base. However, most organizations do not know when, where or how to start empowering. It begins by teaching employees the importance of empowerment and how it can make an organization better – and subsequently giving that empowerment. Empowered employees will show initiative by taking on and completing tasks without guidance. Consider the following questions:

- Are employees empowered to make decisions?
- Are customers empowered to expect our best?

Relationships

All levels of an organization need to focus on knowing how to create long-term relationships, starting with the front-line employees and ending with the owner/CEO of the organization. If your customers see any disconnect, this can be a problem. Building a butler environment helps your organization provide better service as there is a more knowledgeable staff that is focused on building trust by using

leadership and empowerment skills. Consider the following questions:
- Do we have a strong relationship with our customers?
- How do we build strong/stronger relationships?

Each of the six principles needed to develop butlers asks the reader to consider specific questions. These will be discussed further in this book – and should be explored and considered within your organization. Can you answer each question now? Do you have positive responses already to any or all of the questions? Are you unsure of the answers? These questions are an important part of the process and while they may be challenging to think about, the ultimate goal at the end of creating a butler culture for your company is to know that your answers are pointing you in the right direction.

The Butler Experience is about creating an organizational culture that is able and strong, and committed to providing the best service possible. Having a strong organizational culture built around customer service will make it harder for others to truly compete in your market. The culture will help cultivate your customers – and they will become more like partners than customers in the future. The Butler Experience is truly about loyalty.

The journey is long and tough. It is finding the right people to develop into butlers, and it takes an organization willing to invest in The Butler Experience. I will explain how you can excel in the butler concept, and provide you with the information needed to build and grow your own corporate butler program.

Let's get started.

CHAPTER 3

Meeting The Butler

For a number of years in my career, I traveled extensively for an automotive event management company, which coordinated industry trade shows. These were often trips with long flights, living out of hotels rooms away from my family for days, late nights on show floors – and unpredictable weather and travel in the winter.

It was during a trip to Chicago in early 2010 when I first met the man who would become known as the Butler. Always leery of trips to Chicago in the dead of winter as flight delays or cancellations are the norm when major snow storms come in off Lake Michigan, I was prepared for another tumultuous travel experience. What I was not prepared for was meeting a man who would change my perception of customer service and how an organization can improve its customer service environment.

After landing in Chicago, I quickly found a taxi to take me to the hotel – of course, it was a long and nerve-wracking ride in congested city traffic. While the first thing on my mind was getting into my hotel room and refreshing with a shower, that wasn't going to be possible. I had to get on to the show floor and make sure the clients were set up, happy and there were no fires to put out.

My first stop was at one of our client's booth where I noticed an employee of one of my company's partners who was detailing vehicles. He was young, fit, of medium height and a rather unique-looking gentleman as his hair was spiked and the sides of his head were shaved. He definitely caught my attention in more ways than one.

Despite the unusual hairstyle, he was very professional in his appearance and demeanor. He approached me and I realized that he was a genuine person who took his job seriously, and you could tell he had been working hard. "Hello," I said. "I'm Brian, and I'm the Field Operations Manager."

He shook my hand, and looking at me, said, "Hello, sir. My name is Steven, and it is a pleasure to meet you, sir." He postured himself like a butler, standing with his hands behind his back, professional and pleasant, and looked directly at me when he was talking. Then he said, "If you need anything, please let me know, sir."

After the short introduction, he went right back to detailing automobiles. I was immediately amazed by his work ethic and obvious commitment to doing a good job, and also found myself impressed by his manners and etiquette. He was one of the most humble and polite individuals I had ever met.

Later in the evening, I watch Steven again, and I noticed that his performance exceeded that of my employees. He was delivering service with a passion and consistently communicating with our clients throughout the night. As the night grew even longer, Steven's motivation increased, while my team was dragging.

We were all at a point of exhaustion and really needed to rest, and I told them all to leave for the night. Steven looked at me with a serious look on his face and said, "Sir, I would like to stay and complete the job." I insisted that he needed to get some rest too. In my mind I thought, "Does this guy think he is Superman?" All too quickly, and after only five hours of sleep, it was morning and time to get back to work. I needed my caffeine rush, but unfortunately the coffee stands at the show venue didn't open until 9am.

Suddenly, my need for a coffee fix seemed inconsequential as I realized that before getting his much-needed sleep, Steven had gone to the hotel and laundered the towels used for car detailing, then returned back to the show floor to finish the job. I could not believe it, and from that that point on, I knew I wanted Steven as an employee with our organization.

For the next few years, Steven continued to work with us as an employee of our partner, and finally in 2013, joined the company as a Field Manager. During those years, I continued to watch as Steven built himself into a leader, and further grew our client relationships.

From the start, Steven did everything with excellence, working however long it took to get the job done. He was always willing to serve, always seeking to enhance his skills and knowledge, and when he made a promise or commitment, it was kept.

Steven's commitment to service and style not only quickly endeared him to his fellow team members and customers, and earned him a nickname of the Butler. He was without question an empowered individual and leader who earned so much respect and trust from his fellow employees and from the customers. His skills and commitment to providing an excellent customer experience changed the customer service culture at our organization.

The Butler Experience was born out of Steven's caring, compassion and commitment to his employer and customers. His butler approach to customer service was the reason why customers continued to ask specifically for Steven for years.

This butler approach is a simple concept that organizations can easily adopt. The Butler Experience is built around six core concepts which are: be serving at all times, use knowledge, give trustworthy service, show leadership, and be empowered. All of which can lead to the final concept: building stronger relationships with your customers.

I was inspired to write this book because of Steven and to show how The Butler Experience can change an organization's culture. If an organization focuses on building butlers within their organization, they will build stronger relationships with their customers.

It is time for you to build a butler culture in your organization – and through this book, I will show you how.

CHAPTER 4

Be Serving At All Times

When we think of butlers, we envision hard workers who are serving at all times. They work around the clock to make sure the household is running efficiently, and that they are exceeding the employer's expectations. With butlers, there is a direct focus on serving at all times.

> *"A customer is the most important visitor on our premises; he is not dependent on us. We are dependent on him. He is not an interruption in our work. He is the purpose of it. He is not an outsider in our business. He is part of it. We are not doing him a favor by serving him. He is doing us a favor by giving us an opportunity to do so."*
>
> *Mahatma Gandhi*

The International Institute of Modern Butlers published a professional Butler's Code of Ethics, in which it includes the following about service: "Serve the employer as the employer chooses to be served. Actively seek to determine their preferred style of service, while maintaining a comfortable, safe, and secure environment at all times."

Why not service your customers the way they want to be served?

Throughout my career, I have seen the butler concept noticeably utilized by luxury automotive manufacturers. This happens by bringing the "Butler be Serving at all Times" approach to potential customers as a way to increase sales of their luxury brands at large-scale events such as the Pebble Beach Concours d'Elegance. The manufacturers are serving customers the way they want to be served.

Since 1950, the Pebble Beach Concours d'Elegance has been the premier event that showcases some of the rarest automobiles in the world. If you are an automotive fanatic, then you have dreamt of being a part of this event during your lifetime. Celebrities like Jerry Seinfeld, Jay Leno and Arnold Schwarzenegger always attend this yearly tradition. Automotive companies come prepared to cater to the guests with the finest food, wine, and activities. There are automotive displays that look like mansions and, of course, beautiful models everywhere. It truly is a venue where automobile companies take their service to another level – and the higher standard is the norm and not the exception every year.

So why can't customers experience this type of service every day of the year? Not the food and the wine, but the focus on serving the customer at all times. Offering an experience that keeps customers coming back for more, and even pushes them to tell everyone about your organization, should be the standard.

The problem is that most organizations fail to focus on the importance of serving at all times and generally, employees are not developed with enough training to understand or anticipate their customer's needs. Similarly, organizations are not sufficiently focused on the customer. Customers continue to complain about the service they get, but nothing changes.

Getting your business to be focused on serving at all times is a simple approach, and will require some changes:

1. Organizations must incorporate higher standards within their culture to achieve a high level of customer service.
2. Employees must be more driven to focus on exceeding expectations at all times.
3. Organizations need to implement an added-value opportunity to their services or products.

While each of these changes will enhance customer service, it is important that an organization also spends time tracking results and adjusting their customer service focus appropriately.

ESTABLISHING HIGHER STANDARDS

Welcome to first class! No one likes the general boarding seats on an airplane. The seats are narrow, no leg room and most don't even give you a snack these days. Everyone, including myself, would prefer first class. There are roomier seats, more leg room, free drinks and food. Why not give your customers the first class service? All customers should be treated the same no matter how much they spend at your establishment. My father once told me that the customer who buys a dollar item once a day is as important as the customer who buys a large item once every couple of months. It is not hard to provide higher standards; it just takes the leaders of the organization to establish those standards and make sure the employees understand their importance.

To establish higher standards, a leader should develop and implement a code of standards for everyone to follow within the organization. Ritz Carlton incorporated an approach into their business model, known as the Gold Standards, as a way to establish higher standards. The Ritz Carlton's Three Steps of Service are:

1. A warm and sincere greeting. Use the guest's name.
2. Anticipation and fulfillment of each guest's need.
3. Fond farewell. Give a warm good-bye and again, use the guest's name.

Use these standards as a guideline to follow, but keep them easy for employees to understand and adhere to.

ADD VALUE

On the road, I would often hear stories about Steven and how he was serving at all times. His serving went beyond just our clients. I was once told that at shows and events, Steven would take the time to wipe down all of the product specialists' iPads after being used all day. It was not one of Steven's job duties, but being Steven, he was compelled to do more. He added value to himself and to our organization.

Find a way to add value to your service or products. Many organizations and leaders consider adding value as a detriment – because it may cost the organization money – or they feel the customer will want even more in future. This is not always the case. Organizations and their leaders should implement a value-added approach that will enhance the customers' experience.

Education or hands-on sessions are an effective way to add value at a minimal cost. Home Depot and Lowe's have incorporated this concept into their companies. They offer hands-on events not only for adults, but also now for children on a monthly basis. This approach is designed for the family to spend quality time building something together, while the retailers are creating relationships with future buyers: the children.

Adding value will set you apart from the competition. Make a decision on how you want to enhance your customer's experience. Don't hold back because you feel it could cost too much. Develop a value-added element that has minimal cost to your organization, and a focus on reaching the next generation of buyers.

PROFESSIONALISM

The International Butler Academy is based in the Netherlands and offers a specialized training course in etiquette and protocols. They believe that 60 percent of what is perceived about a butler is based on visual messaging, and that social skills can make or break deals and careers. That belief can be true for any type of business model and individual, not just butlers.

A good example of a business model that demonstrates top notch professionalism is Chick-Fil-A. From the presentation and appearance of their staff to the "it was a pleasure to serve you" good-bye statement, Chick-Fil-A stands out above the rest of the fast food industry. For instance, when the drive-through lane backs up, the stores send cashiers out with iPads to take orders and speed up the process. This type of visual messaging is what will set you apart from the rest to customers. Taking professionalism to the next level is simple, and the four steps below can get you started on the right path.

PROFESSIONAL APPEARANCE

Develop a visual image that lets you stand out from the others. Early in my career, I decided to change our dress code from a uniform to a more upscale look for all important events, including media presentations that are commonplace at major shows. Everyone on our team now wears nice slacks with shirt and tie when working these important events. Have you ever seen an automobile detailer working while wearing a shirt and tie? I can tell you that our clients, potential clients and competitors all noticed, because we stood out above the rest. This is an area that organizations should invest in, not only for customer service, but also for branding purposes.

It is important for an organization to establish appearance guidelines for all staff. Employees must always be presentable in front of the clients, and that means they are well-groomed and nicely-dressed at all time- like a butler, exceeding standards. It is about The Butler Experience.

PROFESSIONAL COMMUNICATION

We all like to hear our name when spoken to. Why do you think Starbucks asks for your name? It takes the customer experience from impersonal to personal.

Ask customers their name. If you are unable to get a name, then address them respectfully with "Ma'am" or "Sir." Steven addressed everyone in that manner, no matter what age they were. No matter how brief, open and end every conversation with comments such as "How can I help you today?" and then "Thank you for your business."

POSTURING

Develop your team to understand body language and posturing when interacting with customers. The objective is for employees to posture themselves in a positive way when dealing with different types of situations.

I personally found Steven's approach the best in every possible situation he encountered. His approach was to stand with hands behind his back similar to a butler, and his stance was open, not closed. Customers felt comfortable being with Steven, and could easily share their thoughts and ideas with him.

Remember, 60 percent of what is believed about a butler is based on visual messaging. Why not make sure your visual messaging demonstrates the butler method? Posturing is very important, and should not be overlooked.

ACTIVE LISTENING

Learn to not answer right away; instead simply listen. Hear what your customers' needs and wants are before you assume what the answers are going to be. Then depending on the situation, address those concerns with positive reinforcement, using comments such as "I understand" or "Not a problem." We tend to want to hear our voices more than we want to listen.

Listening allows you to gain ideas, address problems and develop solutions. Teach your employees the importance of good listening skills and how it will enhance your organization's professionalism – and theirs.

MEETING EXPECTATIONS AT ALL TIMES

Employees must understand the importance of meeting and exceeding expectations every time, and following through on their commitment. We hear the phrase "under-promise and over-deliver" all too often. Don't build a culture around that philosophy. Focus on the approach of always providing top-notch service for your customers.

Staying aligned to the following five methods of meeting expectations will help your staff meet those expectations every time.

EDUCATE YOUR CUSTOMERS

Don't assume that the customer understands everything about your services. Help them understand what to expect throughout the sales or service process. The goal is to get the customer to be a part of the process; in return, it will be much easier for staff to consistently not just meet, but exceed expectations.

DEFINE YOUR SERVICE

Make sure employees have a clear understanding of your service expectations and how they should exceed your customer's needs.

COMMUNICATE

Communicate regularly with your customers on issues such as timelines, policies, and service levels. Customers feel that their situation is more important than anyone else. Be open, follow through on your commitment and communicate regularly.

BE AVAILABLE

Be available for all customers when they have questions or concerns.

ACCOUNTABLE

When mistakes happen, make sure to be accountable for your organization's actions. Apologize and develop a solution to fix the problem immediately.

ANTICIPATING YOUR CUSTOMER'S CONCERNS AND NEEDS

Build your organization with tools and resources that make it easier to anticipate your customer's concerns and needs before they happen. It is essential to train employees on how to handle customer issues and suggestions; however, it is also important to build a system that makes it easy for your customers to share their concerns and needs. Simple enhancements can be made to increase your customer service level immediately and efficiently. The following easy-to-do measures can make a huge difference to your customers.

1. Telephone system-

- Remove the phone tree system and incorporate an individual team to answer the phones. Dedicate a phone line solely to customer needs.

2. Website enhancements-
   - A user-friendly website is a great customer service tool.

   - Develop an FAQ page on your website that provides answers and solutions to common questions. This will help reduce the amount of direct inquiries by customers.

   - Incorporate a live chat feature on the website for additional support.

   - Build a social panel supported by loyal customers. The Walt Disney Company is a great example of an organization that created a platform which enable mothers to get advice from other mothers who previously experienced Disney World. The Disney Company took the time to find knowledgeable past visitors to serve as forum moderators for the site, selecting those individuals who demonstrate excellent knowledge of the Disney Destinations.

By being familiar with specific areas of the Disney culture, the panel members can offer helpful tips and suggestion to other families.

1. Feedback system-
   - Develop a program and/or mechanism that solicits feedback from your customer base.

2. Strategy meeting-
   - Hold a monthly meeting with staff at all levels to get feedback and suggestions. I like having a monthly breakfast club meeting with staff and use it as an opportunity to not only discuss how to improve customer service, but to develop new ways of doing business. It is important to continually ask ourselves, "What do our customers need?" Think of it this way: a customer did not ask Apple to develop a cell phone watch or an iPad. Apple employees anticipated consumer's future technological needs and this foresight resulted in products we all need, and more financial success for the organization.

TRACKING YOUR RESULTS THROUGH THE BUTLER PROGRAM

Building a customer service environment requires leaders to measure their results consistently and constantly.

Organizations that invest money into evaluating customer service are successful in their industry. As discussed earlier, Chick-Fil-A's customer service experience is top-notch – and the organization spends over $1 million each year on evaluating service. That is likely significantly more than most organizations can afford to spend. However, I believe in the following three areas that will help you evaluate, develop and sustain a Butler Experience culture for your organization – and the best thing is, it won't cost you a million dollars!

1. Customer Service Feedback-
   - Incorporate a customer service feedback program within your organization. Track and measure the feedback scores and establish benchmark percentages to achieve for each quarter. The measurement tool should be developed in a simple manner that will get the most immediate response from customers; e.g., online, via email or if a retail establishment, in the store. Give the customer a token of appreciation for taking the time to fill out the survey. The objective is to get feedback from customers who are neutral about your service. This will allow you, as a leader, to identify areas that need immediate attention.

2. Employee Development Form-
   - This helps evaluate employees regularly on their job performance. Organizations typically evaluate

employees only during their yearly review. Continuous training and feedback are important for the ongoing success of the organization and its employees.

Over the years, I've used an employee development form that focuses on key areas such as Knowledge of Work, Quality of Work, Situational Responsiveness, Initiative, Dependability, Leadership, Organization, and Management Skills. While the form is tied to a point scale, employees only see below average, average and above average. The objective is to get the employee focused on what areas to improve – not on the point ranking. Each category provides the employee with written feedback and the last section includes manager-set goals for the employee to focus on before the next feedback session. A benchmark is now set in place and measured on a quarterly basis.

A form like this allows you to further develop the employee's skills and help enhance their interaction with your customers.

3. Customer Service Balance Scorecard-
    - This balance score card has been an important element within the strategic planning foundation of the business world for years. Create a customer service balance scorecard tailored to your organization that can measure important

benchmarks for managers, employees, and the organization itself to achieve. The scorecard should be reviewed at least monthly with the entire organization. It is important to focus on areas that can be measured easily and are possible to achieve. Keep in mind, though, that the objective of The Butler Experience is to develop this culture over time, not overnight.

If there is one takeaway from this chapter, it would be that providing excellent customer service should not be selective and given only to the biggest spender or once a year at the fanciest event. Excellent customer service is a 24/7, 365-day a year privilege that we all inherently should provide to every one of our customers. Like Steven did.

CHAPTER 5

Use Your Knowledge

In the heart of the Great Smoky Mountains lies a small restaurant franchise, a favorite among travelers and residents of the Tennessee-Virginia region; a chain not known by many outside the area. The restaurants are unique edifices, painted blue with a highly visible burger and hot dog structure resting atop the roof that can be seen from blocks away.

> *"If you want to out-perform the competition, you have to out-train them."*
>
> *Thom Crosby, Pal's Sudden Service*

This chain is known as Pal's Sudden Service, founded in 1956 by Pal Berger in Kingsport, Tennessee. A forward-thinking individual in what was a newly emerging quick-service food industry at that time, Pal's vision was to be different from the others. His focus was not fast food, but a business model built around quality, speed of service and exceptional customer service. Pal's Sudden Service is definitely a butler within the food service industry as it was the first restaurant to win the Malcolm Baldridge National Quality Award, and recognized for its achievements in the industry and as a world class organization.

Pal's Business Excellence Institute (BEI), a training division of Pal's Sudden Service, was created to show businesses how to achieve success in a demanding environment.

The Institute's website, http://www.palsbei.com/, details how Pal's Sudden Service compares to global and smaller local restaurant operations, and highlights some of the company's achievements over the years:

1. Same-store sales and market share growth for 32 consecutive years.
2. Service speeds that are four times faster than competitors.
3. Order accuracy that is at least 10 times better than closest competitor.
4. Employee turnover that is one-half of the industry average.
5. Four times the repeat business of the best competitor.
6. One complaint per 3,500 orders – 10 times better than competition.

We all know that good customer service can drive a company's success and consistency in growth, and help maintain a solid reputation. Steven exemplified much of the Pal's Sudden Service philosophy in that he always strived to do not only a better job, but to do his best. He took customer service to his highest level and even made detailing a car an art by wiping it down with one hand behind his back – similar to a sommelier pouring a glass of fine wine.

The success of Pal's Sudden Service didn't happen only due to good company processes and procedures. Its success also happened because of in-house employee training and development – validating that knowledge is a powerful tool among employees that can result in better execution and customer service.

Thom Crosby, president and CEO of Pal's Sudden Service was once asked, "What if you spend all this money training someone and then they leave?" His response, "Suppose we don't and then they stay?"

Employee knowledge is the missing element in most organizations, as many companies place employees into positions with little or no experience. A Deloitte Consulting study shows that 70 percent of employee training occurs informally on the job. Insufficient and ineffective on-the-job training is one of many reasons that customer service can be lacking in organizations. Enhancing the employee's development in a specific knowledge area is essential to an organization's success. Organizations that develop knowledgeable employees are seen as leaders in their industry. Again, Steven was the perfect example of how knowledge equates to leadership. His work ethic was recognized and valued by his fellow employees – and by our company's clientele who depended and relied upon him.

This learning process is simple; however, it requires a commitment from the organization and its employees in order to be successful. To build knowledgeable butlers within an organization, there must be a focus on four important categories: commercial awareness, interpersonal skills, resourcefulness and the ability to reinvent yourself.

COMMERCIAL AWARENESS

Butlers are successful because they possess the knowledge of the business, locale, products, services, and competitors and so on. Do you know how to ensure all employees have a commercial awareness of your industry?

Organizations that fill positions rapidly and send employees out into the field expecting immediate high results are setting themselves, and the employees, up for disappointing results, if not outright failure.

To ensure a stronger more knowledgeable employee base, organizations must commit the time needed to create and develop a training program which supports system-wide objectives and action plans. At the conclusion of the training program, employees should be able to walk away confident that they have the knowledge and skills needed to deal with diverse customer needs and demands.

A good training program should also be built around the employee's ability to understand and demonstrate certain core competencies; e.g., company-specific "certifications" that successfully work within their organization. These core competencies are intended to help employees understand the company's business model and its marketplace. Each competency should have specific criteria expected to be met for completion, and when the employee meets those requirements, he or she is then deemed company-certified within each competency.

Additionally, the corporate training program should require the completion of four major components, which include:

1. Education– the employee studies training materials provided by the company. Depending on the competency, the training material may include documents, videos, pictures, PC interaction, and/or one-on-one or group instruction.

2. Verification– the employee verifies that the information is understood and comprehended.

Verification is accomplished through verbal or written tests.

3. Demonstration– the employee demonstrates and performs the desired behaviors for a specified period of time.

4. Sign off– a sign off is official recognition by leadership that the employee successfully completed training and has met the certification criteria.

With customer demands consistently changing, organizations should develop and implement annual refresher training plans to review critical policies and procedures, and ensure continued relevance. This helps to keep knowledge and customer service skills at peak levels, and also ensures that employees have the skills to evolve successfully throughout a changing environment.

A company that wants its brand and message to resonate throughout the industry and with current and future customers will nurture and guide employees, not only in the new-hire training period, but in organizational-specific ways and during expected times of change.

INTERPERSONAL SKILLS

We all live in an ever-changing, technology-driven world and direct personal contact is rarely the first choice of communication these days. Verbal communication, problem-solving, negotiation and listening skills can be easily lost in a tech-driven world. This can result in an employee's confusion over what the client really wants – and an inability to fulfill their needs.

Organizations must train employees in how to listen to – and understand – the needs and wants of the customers, no matter the form of communication. Let employees know that while their style of communication may not be the same as others from inside and outside of the organization, there are training processes in place. Help employees develop their own communication style that is in line with a high-tech world and that enables them to be successful within the company.

No matter the mode of communication, employees should be given an understanding of the 7 C's of communication that are designed to provide clear interaction with other employees, leadership, customers and vendors. The 7 C's of communication are:

1. Clarity– be clear with your message to customers.
2. Consistency– the message should be consistent to all customers.
3. Consideration– put yourself in their shoes.
4. Confidence– be confident in your communication. Don't demonstrate a lack of knowledge.

5. **Courtesy**– demonstrate a positive and friendly attitude. Listen to your customer's concerns.
6. **Concise**– be to the point. Do not have a bunch of jargon added into your message.
7. **Credibility**– tell the truth and stick to your promise

There is another C which good employers understand and integrate within the company culture – and that is Coaching. Leadership need to coach employees in understanding not just the importance of communication, but how to communicate at their best.

This includes continuous reinforcement that problem-solving, negotiating and listening are forms of communicating. Leadership should develop communication processes that help employees meet and exceed customer service standards, and integrate a discussion of these standards into training and organizational meetings. Emphasizing these processes weekly will enhance employee skills and address other issues that can occur internally.

Help create an ingrained ability within your employees of relating well with others by providing tools to improve communication, and transform an employee with weak interpersonal skills into your very own Steven.

RESOURCEFULNESS

Employees should be expected and encouraged to be resourceful in their jobs. The better they are at what they do and how they do it, the more they are needed – and valued – by your customers. Building a resourceful organization and employees is essential to a successful business. Butlers are very resourceful and their employers depend on them for more than performing basic daily duties.

Strong leaders teach employees more than how to just do the responsibilities of their job – the strong leader also teaches staff about the organization and educates them on their value within the organization. Build a culture that fosters cross training and challenge each staff member to share his or her ideas on how to improve any area within the organization. Encourage staff to be an entrepreneur of your business. Resourceful employees will put your business ahead of the competition – if they work in a company culture that recognizes, values and rewards resourcefulness.

Develop a reward system that promotes a resourceful culture. Carl Wilson, CIO for Marriott, once said, "If you want a resourceful culture, you have to be sure to reward, recognize and compensate resourcefulness. Too many make the mistake of offering incentives to employees simply for maintaining the status quo." Remove the status quo perception from your organization and push your employees to be resourceful.

REINVENT YOURSELF

Throughout history, butlers have reinvented their role. Butlers evolved from having responsibility for the King's wine cellar to managing a household, and in modern times, to serving as personal assistants. In order to stay ahead of the competition, an organization and its employees must also learn how to reinvent themselves. Use your knowledge to push you forward. Best-selling author Andy Stanley said it best:

"What do I believe is impossible to do in my field, but if it could be done, would fundamentally change my business?"

Pal's Sudden Success fundamentally changed its business with its drive-through model. Unlike most fast food drive through experiences, customers at Pal's Sudden Service talk face to face with an employee throughout the entire drive-through ordering process. The customer places an order with one employee, and then moves forward to the next window where money and food are exchanged with another employee. There is a personal connection with customer's every time. The new system saw fewer errors and enhanced Pal's customer service.

Mark Sanborn also explores the concept of reinventing yourself in The Fred Factor, a book that discusses how implementing four basic principles into your life can bring renewed energy and creativity to you, both personally and professionally. One of the principles is learning how to make a real difference every day. The more you practice this one a day philosophy, the more likely it is that you can turn the mundane into the extraordinary. Imagine a renewed focus on improving customer service a little every day and at the same time, reinventing yourself. The impact would be extraordinary.

Reinventing yourself is not hard to do. However, it takes thought and consideration of how to do it well, and how to do it right. I encourage you to do the research and look at a number of what are considered best practices for companies. Then determine which is best to implement within your organization, and do it following the one a day philosophy.

One final encouragement about knowledge: as leaders within your organization, tap into the knowledge of your employees. Open the flow locked within their minds, and encourage new thoughts and ideas, change and suggestions, communication and new ways of understanding, and resourcefulness and ingenuity. As butlers do in their profession, employees armed with knowledge are better able to anticipate a customer's expectations and needs.

Knowledgeable employees are skilled and highly regarded – and like the butler, build trust and confidence with the customer every time.

CHAPTER 6

Trustworthy Service

Trust is more than a word that means so much to everyone. As we grew in age and maturity, trust became an integral part of our lives and relationships. It's a feeling ... an intangible "something" from which we all draw comfort – and causes us concern. It's not unusual for adults to wonder at times, "Can we trust our kids, our co-workers, our employees, our friends – even our spouses or partners?" When trust is broken by someone in our life, it has to be earned back by that person in order to regain faith in that person. Even then, it most likely won't be instantaneous. Rebuilding trust could take days, weeks, months – or even years.

> *"Trust is the glue of life. It's the most essential ingredient in effective communication. It's the foundational principle that holds all relationships."*
>
> *Stephen R Covey*

However, there are times when trust will never return and from that point, the relationship is broken. As in our personal life, trust can be broken within an organization or company – which in turn, can damage the business overall. Earnest Hemingway once said "the best way to find out if you can trust somebody is to trust them."

The statement by Hemingway is not just wise, but definitely spot-on. Without trust, you may be perpetually looking over your shoulder, expecting poor behavior or performance from those behind you – rather than focusing on the good you can see directly ahead. Through the years, I've seen organizations and in particular, companies run by new entrepreneurs, fail to build a culture of trust in the staff. When trust in employees is missing from the start, this hinders a company's ability for strong future growth. A culture of trust is critical to any organization's success.

Employees need to feel trusted by their organization's leaders, not perceived or treated as untrustworthy or less than. When a lack of trust is the momentum behind any or all decisions made by the employer, then company performance will begin to collapse – and so will customer service. Not only creating, but embodying a work culture that embraces trust is critical to any organization's success.

It makes sense that a company wants to hire the best and greatest employees. What doesn't make sense, though, is not letting those same employees get behind the wheel because you don't trust their driving.

Consider this: it's a fair assumption that customers buy your products or services because they have trust in what you're selling. That trust is based on the hard work, honesty, integrity, drive and attention to detail your company offers – and you would like to think that your employees are part of the reason for this earned trust.

Yet you still can't readily transfer the trust your customers have in you to your employees for one primary reason: your staff may not be meeting expectations and this often results in inconsistency.

Robert Eckert, former chairman of Mattel says it clearly, "As you go to work, your responsibility should be to build trust." I believe that responsibility is equally as important for the top leader as it is for the entry level employees – and all others in between.

A company's employees are the ones who can build trust with the customer base – after all, they're generally the front line team that clients interact with most. Having a process in place to ensure trust is vital to any business which wants to succeed, grow and most of all, have satisfied clients.

There are five primary objectives that will help an organization build a climate of trustworthy service:

1. Focus on what was promised.

2. Encourage trust.
3. Be consistent.
4. Hold people accountable and acknowledge them for doing a good (or great) job.
5. Tell the truth.

FOCUS ON WHAT WAS PROMISED

Customers select your business for a reason. They may have found you from an online search, perhaps they drove by the company and noticed it – or better yet, you were recommended to them. They did their job by finding you, now it's time for you to do your job and deliver goods or services based on trust.

Success is about providing trustworthy service every time. Companies will often promise the world to a client, and then fail to follow through on their commitment. We all know what happens next – the customer begins to lose trust and takes their business elsewhere. To your competition.

A promise means a lot to a customer. Steven was a man who every day would promise clients a job well done – and then deliver on that promise. If he said the job would be finished by the morning, it was finished on-time every time. He built trust with clients not only in himself, but also within our organization because of this. For those times when a situation was outside of his control and he could not meet his promise – clients understood because they knew Steven's work ethic and commitment was to doing the best he could at all times.

Your business may also have to break a promise at times due to circumstances beyond your control; however, customers will understand if your typical service performance has been solid.

An article posted online at monster.com validates the value of trust as part of your work culture. The author, Pat Mayfield writes,

"Trust is about reliability and doing the right thing. It's also a big factor that will determine success in your job and your career – especially in a rough business climate where your value as an employee is closely watched.

Do your colleagues, subordinates or superiors perceive you as trustworthy and honest? How do you perceive them? Trust is a characteristic that builds respect and loyalty, as well as a supportive and safe work environment. Distrust increases tension and negative "on guard" behavior, which can erode the spirit of the team and ultimately productivity."

ENCOURAGE TRUST

Demonstrate trust to your employees and let them be who they are – don't create a carbon copy employee culture of "yes men." If you have trained employees well and provided the resources and knowledge they need to do a good job, then they will be able to exemplify your commitment to giving trustworthy service.

Encourage trust in your organization and among all members of the individual teams and/or departments. Over the years, I have personally seen many employees who want to take on more responsibility over other staff, but don't have sufficient trust that their team can get the job done. Leaders must educate their supervisory staff and help them learn to depend on their team and organization. The needs of your customers must be the priority of everyone in the company, not just the individual at the front line.

Mayfield also encourages leaders to be proactive with employees – and by doing so, improve the level of trust within the organization. She offers the following four recommendations:

1. Ask the hard questions to build and protect the company.
2. Listen and consider others' ideas with an open mind.
3. Focus on issues and solutions rather than personalities.
4. Set the example, by being responsible and accountable.

BE CONSISTENT

Building trust is about being consistent. Customers want and expect an organization to be consistent in the delivery of their product or service. Lack of delivery and consistency will most likely result in lost business, a lost customer and possibly even poor ratings online for the world to see. A business' reputation can go downhill today in a relatively short time because of the web, social media, and review sites. Nowadays, more consumers than ever check out review sites for business recommendations and ratings.

Steven's service level was consistent no matter what client he was representing on the show floor. He knew that whether the client was an international industry giant worth billions of dollars or a Mom and Pop business from the Heartland, they each were an important client and would get superb service from him.

Consistency is not selective, Mayfield stresses. "It's not enough to be trustworthy only on Tuesdays and Thursdays," she wrote. Furthermore, consistency is measured in words and behaviors, she believes, and offers the following expectations of consistency.

1. Show up – every day and on time – and stay at least the required hours.
2. Do the work; meet or exceed the job description and company standards.
3. Do what you say you will do. Fulfill your promises.

HOLD PEOPLE ACCOUNTABLE AND ACKNOWLEDGE THEM FOR DOING A GOOD (OR GREAT) JOB.

Trust is hard for many leaders who believe the company's success rests solely on their shoulders. Nonetheless, trust is essential to help an organization grow. If an employee is encouraged and empowered in his or her position to make decisions, then let the employee make those decisions. If the decision was not the right one, then hold them accountable. Be sure, though, that the employee knows upfront the accountabilities that lie within the position.

The goal is not to instill fear that employees will be in "trouble" because of a poor decision. Rather, it is to educate them on how to make a better decision the next time – while also reinforcing that you do indeed trust them to do the job. Encouraging your staff to make a decision is much better than they not do anything. The customer knows the difference and will appreciate the employee's efforts.

Steven was always encouraged to make decisions and was trusted by everyone in the organization. At times, he also made a wrong decision – which he learned from – and that subsequently helped him become a better person and employee. When his decisions were correct, I made sure as his immediate supervisor to acknowledge this with him, many times with an incentive for a job well done. Trust that your employees will perform as expected and make the right decisions, and soon you can see how much your customer service has been enhanced.

TELL THE TRUTH

There was once a small boy who cut down a cherry tree and could not tell a lie to his father. That boy, George Washington, became America's first president and known as the "Father of

Our Country." As a leader, you must build a culture the supports telling the truth.

Your front line employees interact with your customers every day. McKinsey Quarterly states it well, saying that the "spark is sometimes missing between the customer and front line employees." That spark is what changes customers into brand followers and it is also how great companies earn trust. Create that spark in your company culture and with your all the employees.

When something goes wrong, it is essential that your company and employees know they must own up to that decision. Give your employees the authority to fix situations immediately for the customer – and earn or regain trust from the customer. Encouraging a culture of deceit or covering up the problem will only cause more damage. Ensure that all staff understands that holding back or hiding information is a detrimental action and in no way considered problem solving.

Stress to your employees your expectation that they accept responsibility for their actions – and that they never ever lie to a customer. If you are worried as a manager or an organization about trusting your employees, then you are only hurting yourself in the long run. Instead, support them by providing the tools and responsibility to make things right when necessary – that is essential to their success. Employees who know they are trusted find remedying a mistake easier to do – and know that it's part of the job.

Trust is the golden nugget to success within an organization. It is time to let go of control and let your employees take your organization to the next level. Have a little trust.

CHAPTER 7

Leadership

Organizations and their hierarchy are changing – companies must now produce the same – or more – with less; the line between a "manager" and an employee in "leadership" is no longer clearly defined. In fact, a manager and leader are often synonymous in business today.

> *"'Leaders aren't born, they are made. And they are made just like anything else, through hard work. And that's the price we'll have to pay to achieve that goal or any goal."*
>
> *Vince Lombardi*

Rutgers Business School discusses this:

"So does a manager need leadership skills? There was a time when the role of the manager and the role of the leader could be easily separated. In this new economy, there is much more *complexity in the workplace. Managers must do more with less and they must deal with constant change. The skills needed for managers and leaders should no longer be easily separated. Organizations cannot afford to keep managers who don't have leadership skills. "*

How do you tie leadership into the butler concept? It's simple – through quality customer service. However, the ability to take customer service to the next level means creating leaders within your organization. It also means that the organization should help its staff develop into leaders that exemplify the characteristics of excellent customer service. The mantra should be: the focus must not be on ourselves, but on providing the service the customers need.

Simply put, employees need to "buy-in" to the concept that they work in an environment where the primary objective is to serve customers ... by providing quality customer service. Leadership/management must help get them to that buy-in point.

Excerpts from an article at Forbes.com best sums up this crucial philosophy:

"This is one of the reasons that leadership, starting at the top and spreading throughout the managerial ranks, is so crucial in a service organization. Constant reconnection with workers within the organization, is your greatest tool.

The goal? Having people get to work and think, "you know what? Maybe if I didn't have to go to work at all it would be better, but since I do have to work, I like this place. It's healthy, clean, supportive, and engaging. So I'm going to give it my attention, performance, commitment, loyalty, and effort.

Reaching for this state is a central function of a leader in a customer focused organization ... this is because your organization's ability to provide service is overwhelmingly affected by how engaged – how professionally "alive" the employees are who come in contact with customers. Employee engagement, in turn, is propelled by organizational leadership."

These thoughts further demonstrate that leaders not only lead people – they also lead the culture that is focused on customer service and relationships. Some leaders are highly skilled at both facets of leading, while others are strongest in one area or the other. Steven was the kind of leader whose strength was serving clients. He had a keen ability to anticipate their needs, often before the client even had a chance to verbalize – or recognize – those needs.

Are you a leader within your organization? Do you know how to create leaders? Can you identify which types of leaders exist within your organization? Business owners and top executives must ask the following questions of themselves:

1. Do we demonstrate we are leaders in the industry?
2. How do we build leaders?
3. How do we ensure that our leaders can best utilize their individual leadership strengths and skills?

Leadership is an evolution ... of leadership styles, of leadership strengths – and weaknesses, of leadership development and training, of a desire to lead, and so much more. How you implement the process of developing leaders will drive your reputation among clients as an organization that delivers on their promise ... and with great customer service.

Over the years, I have seen leadership become more than managing people, as the Rutgers article excerpts earlier in this chapter indicated. Leaders stand out from the rest in everything they do on a daily basis. While Steven struggled in the realm of managing people, he was focused, and a leader in managing clients, processes and procedures.

There will be different types of leaders in your organization. As an executive or owner, you should not only understand and accept that, but be able to:

1. Identify those with leadership potential.
2. Identify those with leadership skills already in place.
3. Determine the type of leadership role an employee should have.

4. Determine the level of leadership the employee is capable of.
5. Provide a work environment that capitalizes on the potential of each and every employee – which includes appropriate training and nurturing of those skills.
6. Provide a culture that encourages growth and success in leadership.

Employees who possess the skills to lead people and processes should play an important and specific role in your organization – that of mentoring other employees to develop and strengthen their inner workplace skills.

Recapping the points above, positioning employees in the right role within the company requires recognizing those who are skilled and motivated enough to take on a larger role – and providing an internal foundation and culture that encourages and fosters growth. Remember, there are different types of people in an organization – and while not all are driven to lead – all can be driven to succeed!

Let's talk successful business practices that help develop that state of a customer-focused, leadership-based organization, using the Butler Experience as a leadership development tool. There are several ways to achieve this:

10-80-10 LEADERSHIP DELEGATION MODEL

I was introduced to the 10/80/10 model in the early stages of my career and I believe it is a game changer for any business. It is a simple yet effective leadership delegation model that organizations have followed for years – best of all, it can be tailored to the circumstances and needs of virtually any company committed to excellence in leadership and subsequently, customer satisfaction.

The 10-80-10 concept is easy to implement; I've tweaked and modified it over the years to fit my organization – and to develop new leaders. My model has four facets rather than three, and I refer to it as the "Driver" model – obviously correlated to an industry I am strongly affiliated with – automobiles. While the 100 percent collective equation and descriptors can vary from company to company – it can work in virtually any industry, and for any for-profit and not-for-profit entity. What I found works best for me professionally is defining employees as being in one of four categories: in Drive Mode, in Neutral, in Park, or Going in Reverse.

Here's what I've seen through my workplace experiences:
1. **Ten percent are in drive mode-**
    - These are the employees who go above the call of duty for the organization. If you provide them the foundation, they will build the house.

    - These are the leaders– either they came to you with leadership skills that you recognized and strengthened, or the organization provided the capacity and culture for those with unrecognized but innate leadership skills the opportunity to nurture and grow them. As you can imagine, Steven fell within the driver category.

2. **Eighty percent are in neutral-**
   - This is the group of employees who don't get a lot of attention or visibility because they do their job without any problems or complaints. They may appear to not be going anywhere within the company – but what if they want to?

   - These employees are often the backbone of your company– however, do you recognize and reconnect with them? Don't let them be an untapped source of excellence and opportunity for you – integrate concepts of the Butler Experience into regular opportunities for growth, training and advancement of this group of employees. Remember what was stated earlier: while they may not want to lead – they do want to succeed!

3. **One percent is in park-**
   - This small group of employees is perceived as warm bodies simply there to do an immediate job – they

are employees you hired to fill spots quickly on a seasonal or holiday basis. You are not sure what do with them after the rush, but they are getting you through the peak times right now.

- The parked employees generally won't to be a long-term or permanent solution – even though you may not know what they are really capable of. Stop hiring to meet short-term needs, and use a focused approach to hiring these employees. Plan for those seasonal needs ahead of time and get to know more about the candidates. Gauge their strengths and abilities while still in the hiring process – determine if they can be an asset to the company in other ways beyond meeting an immediate need. Organizations tend to overlook the potential of these "warm-body" individuals – and may be missing a diamond in the rough that can truly help the company shine.

4. **Nine percent are going backwards and are stuck in reverse-**
    - They are the employees who won't change because they can't accept change, they exhibit poor behaviors, always need additional guidance – and can disrupt the workplace for other workers overall because of poor performance.

- This is a group where leaders have a decision to make: can this person begin to go forward in the company with encouragement and training – or is it time to replace them with a newer model?

As leaders, your focus should be on bringing more people out of neutral and into drive – reversing the percentages so that there are more drivers than neutrals – and by a significantly higher percentage! You do this by identifying and focusing on the individuals who are in neutral and directing your efforts on developing them into drivers. The higher the driver percentage, the more your organization will grow and exceed in all areas of the business.

The customer-focused and leadership-driven organization will have the highest percentage of top performers – these are the folks two will hold others accountable – and will not accept anything less than perfection.

Working with those leaders who do not accept imperfection and do not believe in a status quo – and again, these are the employees best suited to mentoring others into leaders using their inner butler persona – you will begin to produce more drivers and make positive change for the company.

CORRELATING THE 10-80-10 MODEL TO A BUTLER MENTORING PROGRAM

Developing leaders starts with developing those people within your organization who are mentors. Mentors are the individuals who are known as the drivers in the company – like a butler, they anticipate needs and then meet or exceed them. They lead by example. Mentors demonstrate passion, willingness and an eagerness to grow within the company – they are committed to the organization's success and to serving clients to the best of their capability. They focus on building more butlers organization-wide who also will hold others accountable for maintaining and growing a strong customer service culture.

A successful Butler Mentoring Program will help new and existing employees – especially those in neutral – understand the organization's culture, vision and expectations. There are four simple steps to take for this to happen:

1. Goals and action strategies are created and set in place that must be achieved over time by the new employee. Establish a specific time frame for achievement and stick to it.

2. All goals must be realistic and have a direct impact on the goals of the company – and on the goals and abilities of the employee.

3. There is regular communication between the mentor and employee. This helps not only measure the growth

and success of the employee, but identify and problem-solve any roadblocks or issues that occur.

4. The employee must understand that the mentor's time is important – and all feedback coming from the mentor should be presented to the employee as productive comments rather than criticism.

A butler mentoring program provides new employees with a stronger foundation than a quick orientation and one-time training session would before sending them out on their own. It also allows leadership to either provide more training or as the last resort, termination of current employees who are the reversers – those who are in your company's bottom 10 percent and who just are not cutting it.

Mentors will invest time in developing employees into butlers – and they should be rewarded for their commitment as they are helping the company grow and succeed. One of the best ways to reward mentors who are committed to the company's success is to tie a compensation program into their efforts – and the mentee/employee's development. Trust me; drivers want more drivers on the team. So does the executive office.

The Butler Experience is designed to help develop leadership skills throughout the entire organization. As butlers are considered leaders of the domain they serve, so can be your employees. Through researching and learning more about butlers – and from personal observations of Steven – I determined the following four commonalities that successful leaders learn and follow:

1. They are patient-
   - As in the realm of butlering, each day brings a unique set of challenges to the workplace – and leaders understand and adapt to that. They also visibly demonstrate their capacity for patience to all other employees. As customer service can be both rewarding and frustrating, instilling the concept of patience within every employee is essential to an organization's success. Patience helps everyone deal with tough situations appropriately and accurately.

2. They lead by example-
   - This is not the time for the "do as I say, not as I do" admonition. Don't expect your team to stay and work late if you head out at 4:00 to go play 18 holes. Leading by example means your employees can look at you and say, "Wow, he does it. So can I," and that makes it easy for them to follow, even emulate you. Give your best efforts to the organization and your team. Odds are, they'll give you theirs.

3. They are organized-

- Good organization increases productivity and reduces costs, and builds confidence throughout the team that the job can be done. An organized leader creates a culture of confidence and credibility – and instilling this culture in every member of that team also gives them a leg up on those who are not so organized. Why? Because the entire team isn't wasting time and energy trying to sort out the disruption.
- If organization is not your strongest suit, however, don't despair. Build that organizational culture by delegating to those team members who have demonstrated organizations skills. Let them know what you want and expect – and then let them deliver for you.

4. They have a teamwork-focused approach-
    - Identifying and calling upon the strengths of individual team members to offset any you may not have is one example of the whole team coming together for the common good: top-notch customer service, building a strong team and helping the company grow. While a butler may get the visibility and recognition for the household running smoothly, we all know he or she didn't do it alone. It takes everyone to make the team successful – and

it takes the entire team to make The Butler Experience work in your organization.

E+R=O

Another resource for developing leaders within your organization is the E+R=O – Event + Response = Outcome Formula. I personally attest to and adhere to this concept, which I first learned about when reading Jack Canfield's The Success Principles – and I've seen the formula evolve throughout the years. In fact, E+R=O is now used by The Ohio State University football Buckeyes as a way to increase leadership development among members of the team.

Think about this ... every year, a class of football recruits enters the hallowed halls of OSU's Horseshoe Stadium – knowing that they are there to do as well as, if not better than, last year's players – many who were team leaders and now playing professional football, on to new careers or in grad school.

How do you build new leaders to replace those who have moved on? How do you get the new members to respond positively and appropriately? How do you get them to step up? How do you dispel their sense of being "new to the team" or a nervous about the big shoes left to fill?

It starts with changing their behaviors, their thoughts and the way they communicate. They need to learn how to look at situations differently and then learn to respond appropriately.

E+R=O is a basic and simple approach that will bring both personal and professional reward. It is not a quick fix, and it requires looking within yourself and your attitudes. We all have good and bad circumstances in our lives. How we respond to these experiences can impact how these experiences affect us. While we can't always control the outcome – what we can control is our response – and how we respond can dictate how we live our life.

The same with how we lead. Leadership is about responding positively and appropriately when times get down and dirty. Introducing the E+R=O formula to your employees will help them change the way they think, behave and communicate in the future. Become a true leader by removing the bad habits that are controlling your life, by not complaining – and focusing on how your response affects not only you, but all those around you.

Leadership skills and knowledge gained through the Butler Experience happen over time. It is an ongoing process that becomes ingrained within those employees willing to learn and grow – and it is a process built on trust and openness. Employees learn they are valued by leadership, and that they have a mentor to turn to with questions, concerns or suggestions.

Simply stated, leadership is learned and earned – not given.

CHAPTER 8

Empowerment

It is intriguing to see that empowering employees is often an ongoing challenge of leadership within organizations. Many leaders are unaware of the importance of empowerment and how it can make the organization better. Some are concerned that by empowering their employees, there will be costly mistakes to the organization. There is also the perception that some customers will try and take advantage of the company, raising concern among leadership that the empowered employee may not always recognize that customer looking to get something for nothing. Some leaders also feel threatened about their own job security, and that fear prevents them from empowering employees.

> *"As we look into the next century, leaders will be those who empower others."*
>
> *Bill Gates*

That doesn't have to be the case. Employees who are empowered are happier in their jobs and feel they are making a difference to their employer – and helping their boss.

More than once, this book discusses similar traits between a butler and a good customer service professional; it's a concept worth repeating. Would you hire a butler for your household and not give that individual the empowerment to make decisions? Of course not. After all, butlers are expected to make decisions and handle issues that arise by making an independent and empowered decision. Ask yourself then, "Why am I not also empowering employees?" Instilling an empowerment mindset into employees is a struggle to most leaders for a very basic and simple reason: they do not know where or how to start empowering employees.

I find myself looking for butler's every time I go into a business. As Steven's leader, I empowered him to make decisions that were in the best interest of our organization. I was confident that he would make a decision he felt was right at any given time. While it was not uncommon to hear him say, "it is better to make a decision now and ask for forgiveness later," I cannot remember a decision he made that was wrong or out of line.

It is easy to see why some organizations are at the top of their industry and how empowered employees make a difference in their business culture, including to the bottom line. The benefit of empowering employees is that it allows them to create strong, long-term relationships with your current and future client base. Empowered employees show initiative by taking on and completing tasks without guidance.

Finding more employees today like Steven is a struggle, to say the least.

EMPOWERED DAVID

During a recent visit to a hardware store, I was assisted by an employee, David, who reminded me of Steven. It was around 7 a.m. on a fall Saturday morning, and I was up early to tackle a job that is always a needed to clear an area in my yard that was full of bushes, trees and grass – all of which had to be cut down and removed. The day was nasty and it was raining non-stop, but I was determined to complete the job within four hours. That goal was definitely ambitious, but it was Saturday – and I fully intended to be done and in front of the television, ready for a noon kickoff of college football.

I made it to Home Depot, where David helped me and set me up with the equipment. He was very professional, described everything in detail and in my opinion, went above and beyond to make sure I was ready for my "adventure."

I spent hours working on the jungle of grass and brush, most of which was about six feet high. The brush hog's tires were spinning non-stop, spraying mud from the deluge of rain. I realized that the job was going to take much longer than anticipated. I decided to make a cut through a rough hilly area, and as the brush hog was going downhill, I was having a hard time keeping it under control. The equipment was dragging me down the hill at a fast rate of speed – and the brush was cutting me everywhere it could. Suddenly I hit a ditch, the brush hog was stuck and a tire had fallen off. What else could go wrong? I was having a difficult time getting the machine out the ditch and finally succeeded in pulling it out with my truck. Thankfully, two friends were able to help me get the machine back into the truck so I could take it back.

I returned to Home Depot, looking like I had gone 10 rounds with the brush hog and told David what had happened with the machine. He said, "I have never had a tire fall off before. Would you be interested in another machine?" Now that was a crazy question to ask because I was finished. I also am not so proud to hold the distinction of being the first guy to ever make a brush hog lose its tire. With a smile, I simply answered, "Nope. This job needs a bigger machine," and he laughed.

Done with the project for the day, I told David to take the equipment rental charge out of my $150 deposit, to which he said, "No problem." He then gave me a receipt, telling me that that he had refunded the full deposit amount, adding, "You have had a rough day, so I refunded your money." I was amazed and could not believe what had just happened. This employee was empowered to make a decision without management approval and did it on his own.

It was a job I never want to repeat. I was covered in mud and missed the kickoff! However, looking back, I realize that this empowered employee made a bad day so much better.

This home improvement company has a great philosophy. An article in Fortune Magazine shared some interesting background about Home Depot. The company was founded on the philosophy of empowering its employees, but later struggled to maintain that culture when it began to focus on increasing sites outside the U.S. The expansion growth started to negatively affect the employees of the organization, and this trickled down to the customers. Frank Blake, CEO of Home Depot, quickly realized that the company needed to return to its empowered employee culture. The change made a difference as the retailer began to see a return to higher profits and a more loyal customer base.

This empowerment belief was what I noticed during my visits to Home Depot on that day. As a customer, it changed my perception of Home Depot, which by the way, is now my preferred home improvement store. I never imagined – or expected – that the clerk would refund my money, and it made me think of Steven. Having the freedom to make a decision is empowerment, and empowering employees is a rewarding experience for your customers. You can do this simply by changing your culture and focusing on four simple but powerful behaviors to increase empowerment within the workplace.

OPEN COMMUNICATION

It is impossible to say how many times I have heard organizations and leaders state they have an open door policy. Do they really? Can you honestly say that your employees are able to voice anything that is on their mind? Usually they won't.

Leaders may say they are open to communication, but truly do not come across as willing to have an open door (or ear) to communication. There is often a fear among employees that open communication is perceived as complaining and negative, an could result in disciplinary action. A good leader creates an environment that encourages employees to share positive and solution-driven communication, and eliminates that fear.

As a leader, listen to – and hear – what employees have to say, whether positive or negative. Then find a way to use the conversation as an opportunity to improve the organization. Former U.S. Secretary of State and retired 4-Star General Colin Powell once said, "The day soldiers stop bringing their problems is the day you have stopped leading them. They have either lost confidence that you can help or concluded you do not care." Seek out the communication in your organization and you will see a difference in how your employees respond.

THE ABILITY TO EXPERIMENT

All too often, employees are afraid or too nervous to experiment. Not allowing employees to experiment fosters a status quo mentality. Employees who experiment will share innovative and creative suggestions for the good of the organization, and can offer operational solutions for issues in the organization.

Management guru Tom Peters often shares a story about a Fed Ex employee who had the ability to experiment when a tower went out of commission as the result of a snow storm. The tower served FedEx's main call center and the phone company was unable to get to the top of the mountain to repair it in a timely matter. A FedEx technician, without any direction or approval from upper management or the phone company, chartered a helicopter to fly him to the top of the mountain so he could fix the tower. This employee's decision allowed the company to quickly resume its normal operations. While this is a pretty unique example of experimenting, the decision made by this Fed Ex employee fits perfectly within the company's beliefs. FedEx's People Philosophy states, "The people priority acknowledges the importance of employee satisfaction and empowerment to create an environment where employees feel secure enough to take risks and become innovative in pursuing quality, service and customer satisfaction."

The risk taken by one employee ended up being a reward for the organization. Driving excellent customer service is built around the ability to experiment. Employees who experiment are focused on always improving and exceeding customer expectations – and problems immediately become solutions without the red tape. Products and services improve, and organizations can find they are ahead of the competition. Amazon CEO Jeff Bezos sums it up best, "If you double the number of experiments you do per year, you're going to double your inventiveness."

Before taking the company public, Google founders Larry Page and Sergey Brin included a letter in an annual report outlining Google's strategies. The letter discussed a workplace philosophy of allowing employees to spend the equivalent of one day during the work week to "experiment" by pursuing ideas and projects that they strongly feel would benefit the Google enterprise. Several products were developed from experimentation that enhanced Google's consumer offerings – products that were not created or launched using external resources.

Instill the opportunity to experiment within your company's culture. Leaders should allocate two to four hours each week for their employees to experiment – and encourage this experimentation. Fostering an environment that allows employees to bring their ideas to life will help companies be more innovative and competitive in their industry for years to come. This also provides further validation that employees are a valuable resource.

DECISION-MAKING FREEDOM

It is important for leaders of organizations to realize that no decision is a wrong decision. Employees must have the freedom to make decisions. Ritz-Carlton is a leader in the hotel industry, known and respected for their luxury and customer service. A major reason for this success is that their employees have the freedom to make decisions. Every employee at every level is empowered to spend $2,000 per guest per day, if needed to engage with guests. Joseph Quitoni, Corporate Director for Ritz-Carlton, explains that it is not about money, but about the ability to connect with guests and leave a customer service imprint that is unique, memorable and positive.

In customer service, decisions are made daily by employees at every level within the organization. How employees are empowered in decision-making determines if it is good or bad for the organization. Budget a certain amount of dollars that allow employees to enhance their customer's experience. Give them the freedom to make fiscally responsible decisions for the organization.

TEAM-APPROACHED EMPOWERMENT

Team approached empowerment allows team members to assume full responsibility for the quality of their work while planning, controlling, improving and implementing their own work process. The intent is for teams to work together to quickly address customer issues.

This is not a new concept. Many organizations see tremendous success when employees are involved in the daily management of the business as members of a work team. A 1995 article published in Quality Digest, "Self-Directed Work Teams: A Competitive Advantage," shared how work teams made a big difference for 3M. The article stated that 3M's facility in Hutchinson, Minn. saw increased production gains of 300 percent through team-approached empowerment. Their team-approached empowerment helped lower operating costs, increased productivity and decreased cycle times.

Team-approached empowerment takes time to implement within an organization. The process starts as leaders of the organization form teams and allows each member to be part of the decision-making process. An organizational-wide strategy must be formed that focuses on team-approached empowerment. To be successful, the strategy must allow teams to experiment, openly communicate, and have the freedom to make decisions.

In order to achieve a team-approached empowerment culture, an organization and its management must also look at employment issues differently, including policies and procedures, incentives and recognition. Understand that the approach is no longer on the individual, but on the team as a whole. The time expenditure will be outweighed by the apparent increase in employee motivation and commitment.

Employees will begin to feel more valued, and validated that they are truly making a difference in the organization.

Empower your butlers to make a difference starting today. Do not stifle their ability to experiment, speak openly, and make decisions individually or with their team.

CHAPTER 9

Relationships

Creating relationships within a business culture is professionally and profoundly personal.

Staff at every rung of the ladder within an organization must always be focused on creating strong and lasting external relationships with customers/clientele, starting at the first step of the ladder all the way up to the very top.

> *"Succeeding in business is all about making connections."*
>
> *Sir Richard Branson, Founder of the Virgin Group*

Relationships should also be forged internally within the company – with cooperative collaboration rather than cutthroat competition the driving force behind providing quality customer service. After all, team members are dependent upon the entire team for success. Bear in mind that this discussion of collaboration is directly related to serving the customer, not meeting sales quotas; the two are mutually exclusive.

If your customers see any disconnect between external relationships; e.g., their own relationship with one or more employees – and/or internally, between two or more employees with obvious discord or inability to communicate with each other, well ... that can be a challenge. There will be problems with how clients perceive your employee's commitment and ability to building a lasting relationship – both personally and professionally – and this can skew their confidence in the company itself.

In Chapter 2, I introduced the B-U-T-L-E-R acronym with a brief overview of each letter and its overall relationship to the book. In this chapter, I will elaborate more on Relationships – and how they can help – or hinder – the company's success.

When it comes to customer service, size doesn't matter. Providing top-notch customer service is just as important to a small Mom and Pop business as it is to a Fortune 500 company. Amazon is a prime example that no company is too big to not care about the level of customer service it provides. In February 2016, the Nielson Company, which owns and conducts the Harris Poll®, issued its annual list of top ten companies for solid corporate reputation – which includes customer service as one of its criteria. Amazon topped the list – and this was the eighth consecutive year that Amazon was in the top ten.

Amazon topped another list in August 2015 as reported in USA Today: it made the 24/7 Wall St. Customer Service Hall of Fame – Amazon's sixth consecutive year topping the list. The article cited Amazon's "self-described customer obsession" as a major factor. "We're not competitor obsessed, we're customer obsessed," said Amazon CEO Jeff Bezos – explaining that the culture is company-wide, across all departments from top to bottom.

You don't have to be a corporate giant like Amazon to bring a similar level of quality customer service relationships to your organization – and if you focus on the following three key areas, you can be well on your way.

DETERMINE THE STRENGTH OF THE RELATIONSHIP WITH YOUR CUSTOMERS.

1) Through communication-
   - Do your employees reach out to customers only when it's time to make another sale? Sharing news or information about the company with customers is a great way to stay in touch and let customers know you think about them at other times.

2) Sharing Information-
   - Do employees listen as well as tell? Do they know names and faces? Is there a human connection between employees and those customers who want

to talk about their children, their recent vacation, an accomplishment in their job – and vice versa – can the interested customer learn more about the employee?

3) **Is the relationship built around we?** -
   - For instance, does your company offer a rewards or customer loyalty program? Such programs enhance the customer's relationship with your staff and ultimately helps create a bond with the company. Treating the customer as a partner rather than an entity from which you will make a sale enhances the "we" aspect of a relationship.

Gauge the strength of the relationships your staff has with customers/clients – and find out what particular strengths work best and then determine how to instill these strengths in all employees. Steven was an open book and clients always felt comfortable getting to know more about him – and he had a key sense of which clients wanted to be asked about their lives as well – and which didn't.

On the flip side, if there seem to be problems with customer service relationships, it's important to also identify what the weaknesses are – and then address and resolve those weaknesses. If there is a problem, acknowledge it, apologize for it – and then find a solution. Simply saying "I'm sorry, but that's our policy and we can't do anything" is not going to cut it – and probably will lose the customer for you. There goes that relationship!

Understand that it's not the company which builds the relationship – it's the people at the company – and they are the ones responsible for managing those relationships. If that means training and retraining is needed among staff, then train and retrain staff as needed.

It's also important to keep in mind that customers do talk to each other and while recommendations can help make the company, bad reviews and comments about poor customer service can break it. In Bezos' 7 Customer Service Lessons, it's said that unhappy customers in the "real world" may tell six friends about their negative experience – while unhappy customers posting about their experience online may each reach 6,000.

ENCOURAGE TEAM MEMBERS TO BUILD STRONG RELATIONSHIPS AND EXCEED EXPECTATIONS

1) Clarify expectations-
    - Whether the company owner or department manager, set clear expectations and guidelines related to your customer service strategy. By emphasizing the importance for all employees to create and maintain good internal and external relationships, customer service is enhanced – and that can help drive repeat business from customers.

2) **Don't offer anything you can't deliver on-**
   - This can't be said any clearer than this: don't promise something you can't do. Customers would rather be told honestly that their order can't be shipped overnight, but it will go out on a certain day. If you tell them otherwise, you will have lied – and the customer will eventually know that.

3) **Be invested in their success-**
   - Let your company be a resource and value-added entity – offering information and suggestions that can meet the clients professional or personal needs. Is there a free workshop coming up that would help with a recent product the customer purchased? Do you offer in-house training for equipment the customer purchased from you? Doing this at no cost to the customer strengthens your relationship – and is a good way to help ensure customer retention.

4) **Stay Connected-**
   - Again, communication should not be limited only to an order or repeat sale. Whether in person, over the phone or by email, staying connected with a client will keep that relationship connected too. It

helps to also find out the client's preferred method of contact – and shows you value their time, too.

The suggestions above can be considered as sales equity, which is a tool for growth – both for your company and for your customer. Helping customers enhance their relationship with you, beyond the products and services you sell, solidifies your corporate reputation as one that provides a great customer service experience.

PERSONALIZE YOUR RELATIONSHIP EXPERIENCES – AND COLOR OUTSIDE THE LINES.

1) **Break the rules now and then-**
   - Give a little something extra to the customer. The burger normally gets one pickle – give them two! Create a white-glove program that denotes luxury service to the customer, but adds no additional cost or time to the overall experience.

2) **Don't wait for the new co-worker to come to you-**
   - Get to know those you work with. Ask to sit down with them in the cafeteria – create an ally, not an adversary.

Steven personalized every relationship, adding special touches to enhance the external customer experience and create an internal level of comfort and trust among his fellow workers.

It's worth repeating once again that the following are vital components to building strong customer service Relationships and should be considered as an integral part of the customer service culture:

1) Be Serving At All Times- Focus on giving customers your best every time, with a demonstrated willingness to serve to the best of your ability – this helps maintain a strong and mutually-respectful relationship.

2) Use Knowledge- Demonstrate that the organization and staff has the knowledge to meet and even exceed the needs of its customers. Through continued training, knowledge is enhanced – and relationships strengthened.

3) Trustworthy Service- Is your word golden to all customers? Do they trust you will do what's been promised? Do you need to enhance that trust? Again, don't over-promise and under-deliver. That destroys trust immediately, and quickly kills a relationship – and loses business.

4) Leadership- Is the company recognized as a leader in its industry? Is the company culture indicative of good

leadership? Are employees empowered to be leaders and can they lead by example – especially for the good of a client? Employees who can acknowledge and meet a client's realistic needs and expectation are good leaders – and help keep that relationship solid.

5) Empower- Are employees empowered to make decisions and provided with the tools and resources to act in the customer's best interests? The employee who can make a decision that meets the customer's needs at any given time sends the message that customers are empowered to expect the best – and that they and the company appreciate the relationship.

6) Relationships- Are your employees building strong lasting relationships? Relationships are an integral part of the customer service culture. Understand that it's not the company which builds the relationship – it's the people at the company – and they are the ones responsible for managing those relationships.

An organization which is unable to understand its relationship with customers will also find it difficult to maintain its visibility among a potential client base – and will most likely find growing the company a challenge.

The organization which understands the importance of solid relationships both internally and externally encourages their team members to create, nurture and grow relationships with clients and fellow staff members. The employee's level of professionalism in demeanor and dress, communication skills, the ability to problem solve, flexibility and overall engagement with the customer are all key components of a strong, lasting and mutually-beneficial relationship.

I offer a final parting comment from Amazon CEO Jeff Bezos, "It's easy to listen to customers. However, the first step of every employee must be to understand them and their needs in order to successfully better the organization."

CHAPTER 10

Butler Culture

If there is one primary message within The Butler Experience, it would be to create an organizational culture that cares about providing the best service possible. Every time. Once implemented into your organization, this culture will also become ingrained into your customers – and they will become more as partners than customers in the future.

> *"We believe that customer service shouldn't be just a department; it should be the entire company."*
>
> *Tony Hsieh, Zappos CEO*

Several other key messages also resonate within this book – and it is my hope that readers have gained new and inspiring knowledge from these messages.

Focus on building an organization that provides better service with a more knowledgeable staff – employees who are centered on building trust through their leadership and empowerment abilities. These focused behaviors will help build stronger relationships with your current and potential client base. The result?

You will see a deeper loyalty from your employees and clients, and the strong customer service culture will make it harder for competitors to succeed in your market.

The journey can be long and challenging, but it is not impossible. It means finding the right people to build into butlers, and an organization's commitment to invest time, energy and resources into making The Butler Experience work for them. The Butler Experience can only be successful when it is ingrained into the organization's daily activities and becomes an inherent part of its culture. The entire organization must be "all in" to make The Butler Experience work. All levels of an organization need to focus on creating long-term relationships, starting with the front line employees and ending with the owner/CEO of the organization.

Leaders, it is your job to continually communicate about and promote The Butler Experience as an expectation and inherent part of every job, and to keep it in front of employees each day. It should be deeply instilled into every internal employee program, including mentoring and training, team meetings, incentive and reward systems, and so on. Customers should then notice a change in the level of service they get –

and employees will feel the energy of the program, and pride in their success.

I personally attest to the tremendous benefits that come from living The Butler Experience. My own organization's culture has changed throughout the last year because we practice what is preached. Our employees are focused on this program, and as a leader, I advocate for it every day. Employees carry business cards with our customer service mission, goal and behaviors, and I often hear employees ask others if they have their cards on them. Our level of service continues to change for the better. We are no longer concerned just about getting the job done – we are driven to make a difference. We are developing into a stronger team, and everyone that joins our team is aware of our expectations and of this new culture. The Butler Experience has made it easier to hold everyone accountable within the organization.

Steven is no longer with us in this world, but his spirit lives on through The Butler Experience. I miss Steven and am grateful for the short time that he was a part of my life. He truly changed the way I view customer service both personally and professionally. It is because of Steven that I have the opportunity to share The Butler Experience with you. Use the tools contained throughout this book to develop a butler culture within your organization. Before you know it, there will be several Stevens on your team.

As I close, it is important to understand that change will not happen overnight. However, with a commitment to the plan, you will soon see the evolution of a different organization – one that is focused on providing excellent customer service to every customer ... every time.

It only takes one Butler to get it started ... and that is you.

Bibliography

Page 1
"Bad Customer Service Costs Businesses Billions Of Dollars,"
Shep Hyken- http://www.forbes.com/sites/shephyken/2016/08/27/bad-customer-service-costs-businesses-billions-of-dollars/

Page 6
The Skyscraping Cost of Bad Customer Service, Geoff Weiss – https://www.entrepreneur.com/article/232580, (March, 2014)

Page 1 & 7
"Customers 2020 - the future of B-2-B customer experience," http://www.walkerinfo.com/customers2020/, (September 2014)

Page 9
"Southwest Airlines motivates its employees with a purpose bigger than a paycheck,"
http://www.forbes.com/sites/carminegallo/2014/01/21/southwest-airlines-motivates-its-employees-with-a-purpose-bigger-than-a-paycheck/ (January 21, 2014)

Page 10
Infographic, "The Importance of Employee Engagement," http://www.dalecarnegie.com/employee-engagement/engaged-employees-infographic/ (July 2014)

Page 12
"Want your Company to Succeed in the Future? Invest in Employee Skills Training ..." Lisa Quast- http://www.forbes.com/sites/lisaquast/2012/05/14/want-your-company-to-succeed-in-the-future-invest-in-employee-skills-training-like-deloitte-llp/, (May 14, 2012)

Page 13
Covey, Steven M.R., *The Speed of Trust: The One Thing That Changes Everything* (New York: Free Press 2008)

Page 22
The International Institute of Modern Butlers, Teaching Right Mindset, People-skills, & Superior-service Expertise
http://www.modernbutlers.com/

Page 23
Pebble Beach Concours dElegance Event,
http://www.pebblebeachconcours.net/

Page 25
Ritz Carlton's Three Steps of Service,
http://www.ritzcarlton.com/en/Corporate/GoldStandards/Default.htm

Page 27
International Butler Academy Etiquette and Protocols,
http://www.butlerschool.com/en_US/specialized-training/etiquette-and-protocol/

Page 27
"Chick-fil-A's Recipe for Customer Service, Fast Company, http://www.fastcompany.com/resources/customer/chickfila.html

Page 33
A lesson in customer service from Chick-fil-A President Dan Cathy, SAS Insights, http:/www/sas.com/en_us/insights/articles/marketing/a-lesson-in-customer-service-from-chick-fila-html

Page 38
Malcolm Baldridge National Quality Award 2001, National Institutes of Standards and Technology, http://www.nist.gov/baldrige/

Pal's Business Excellence Institute, http://www.palsbei.com/

Page 39
Thom Crosby response about training, "Suppose we don't and then they stay?" http://www.inc.com/audacious-companies/leigh-buchanan/pals-sudden-service.html

Deloitte Consulting Study on Employee Training, http://maamodt.asp.radford.edu/Aamodt%20(5th)/Case%20Study%20Articles/Case%20study%20-%20Pal's%20Sudden%20Service.

Page 45
Quote by Carl Wilson, CIO for Marriott, https://books.google.com/books?id=IA0AAAAAMBAJ&pg=PA46&lpg=PA46&dq=resourceful+employee+quotes&source=bl&ots#v=onepage&q=resourceful%20employee%20quotes&f=false

Page 46
A quote by Andy Stanley
http://www.goodreads.com/quotes/668273

Page 46
Sanborn, M. (2004). The Fred Factor. London: Random House Business.

Page 53-55
Six Steps to Building Trust in the Workplace, http://www.monster.com/career-advice/article/6-steps-to-building-trust-in-the-workplace-hot-jobs

Page 57
"The 'Moment of Truth' in Customer Service, http://www.mckinsey.com/business-functions/organization/our-insights/the-moment-of-truth-in-customer-service (February 2006)

Page 59
"Do we need managers with leadership skills?" Rutgers University
http://www.business.rutgers.edu/executive-education/blogs/do-we-need-managers-leadership-skills

Page 60-61
Leadership, Service And Sustaining The Customer Experience
Micah Solomon –
https://www.forbes.com/sites/micahsolomon/2014/12/07/customer-experience-leadership-leading-for-employee-engagement-and-sustainably-great-customer-service/#37b9a4b85635

Page 72
"Changing How You Work: Using the E+R=O Formula, http://intentionalworkplace.com/2010/09/23/changing-how-you-work-using-the-ero-formula/

Page 74
Bill Gates quote, http://www.bizjournals.com/bizjournals/how-to/growth-strategies/2014/12/employee-empowerment-and-business-success.html?page=all

Page 78
Fortune Magazine, "Home Depot knows when to call it quits, http://fortune.com/2012/10/26/home-depot-knows-when-to-call-it-quits/, (Oct. 26, 2012)

Page 80
Tom Peters recounts story about FedEx employee and a helicopter rental,
http://www.sumptionandwyland.com/index.php?option=com_content&task=view&id=39&Itemid=56&rid=15

Page 81
Google gives employees 20 percent of work week to experiment: Google investor section
https://investor.google.com/corporate/2004/founders-letter.htm

Page 82
Decision-making freedom, Ritz Carlton
http://ritzcarltonleadershipcenter.com/tag/employee-empowerment/

Page 83
"At 3-M, employees join together to manage their daily work through self-directed work teams,
http://m.qualitydigest.com/self-directed-work-teams-competitive-Advantage.html

Page 87
2015's Customer Service Hall of Fame,
http://www.usatoday.com/story/money/business/2015/07/24/24-7-wall-st-customer-service-hall-fame/30599943/   (August 2, 2015)

Page 86-87

Amazon ranked most reputable company in U.S. in Harris Poll
http://www.upi.com/Top_News/US/2017/02/20/Amazon-ranked-most-reputable-company-in-US-in-Harris-Poll/6791487617347/

Page 89

7 Customer Service Lessons from Amazon CEO Jeff Bezos
https://www.salesforce.com/blog/2013/06/jeff-bezos-lessons.html

Entire Book- Quotes
Popular Quotes
https://www.goodreads.com/quotes

Index

10-80-10 63-64
3M 83

A
Apple
  iPad 26
  technology 33
Amazon 86-87

B
Bezos, Jeff 81, 87, 89, 94
Blake, Frank 78
Branson, Sir Richard 85
Brin, Sergey 81

C
Canfield, Jack 72
Carnegie, Dale 10
Chick-Fil-A 27, 33
Crosby, Thom 37, 39
Covey, Stephen R 49

D
Deloitte Consulting 12, 39

E
E+R=O 72-73
Entrepreneur 6
Eckert, Robert 13, 51

F
Fed Ex 81
Forbes
  loss business 1
  Southwest Airlines 9
  leadership 60-61
Fortune 78, 86
Fresh Prince 5

G
Gallup 11
Gandhi, Mahatma 22
Gates, Bill 74
Google 81

H
Harris Poll 86
Hemingway, Earnest 50
Home Depot
  education 26
  Frank Blake 78
  store associate 76-78
Hsieh, Tony 95
Hyken, Shep 1

I
Intl Butler Academy 27
Intl Inst. of Modern Butlers 22

L
Leno, Jay 23
Lombardi, Vince 59
Lowes 26

M
Malcolm Baldridge 38
Mattel 13, 51
Mayfield, Pat 53-55
Marriott 45
McKinsey Quarterly 57
Mr. Belvedere 5

N
Nielson Company 86

P
Page, Larry 81
Pal's Business Institute 38
Pal's Sudden Service 38-39, 46
PebbleBeach Concours D'El. 23
Peters, Tom 80
Powell, General Colin 79

Q
Quitoni, Joseph 82

R
Rutgers Schl of Business 59, 62
Ritz Carlton 25, 82

S
Sanborn, Mark 46
Seinfeld, Jerry 23
Schwarzenegger, Arnold 23
Southwest Airlines 9
Stanley Andy 46

T
The Ohio State Buckeyes 72

V
Virgin Airlines 85

U
USA Today 87

W
Walker Consulting 1, 7
Walt Disney 32
Washington, George 56
Wilson, Carl 45

Z
Zappos 95

The **BUTLER EXPERIENCE**

About Author

Brian Rowland has over 18 years' experience in corporate operations and leadership positions, with demonstrated success in conceptualizing, developing, and managing operations; aligning strategic initiatives for business development; and revenue generation and growth. He has a proven record of significant organizational management with expertise in strategic planning, operations management, and client relationship management.

Throughout his career, Brian has been recognized as a visionary business strategist with proven successes in driving revenue growth, accelerating employee performance, managing multi-million dollar P&L budgets, and maximizing shareholder value in competitive industries. He demonstrates a discerning sense of organizational efficiency coupled with cross-functional leadership and innovative solutions development. His interactive, motivational, and decisive management style has enabled him to drive business growth, institute streamlined processes and procedures, deliver customer service excellence and generate synergy across systems, teams, and businesses.

He holds a Master of Business Administration with a specialization in applied management from Indiana Wesleyan University, and earned a Bachelor of Science in organizational management from Tusculum College in Tennessee. Additionally, he is a member of the adjunct faculty with the University of Phoenix and has over several years' experience presenting master lectures on Operations Management, Strategic Planning & Implementation, Resource Optimization, Strategies for Competitive Advantage, and Strategies Implementation and Alignment.

Made in the USA
Lexington, KY
28 December 2018